KU-600-687

THE BATTLE FOR THE ETHERIC REALM

THE BATTLE FOR THE ETHERIC REALM

Moral Technique and Etheric Technology
Apocalyptic Symptoms

Nick Thomas

TEMPLE LODGE
London

Translated from the German by J. Collis

This book is based on transcripts (edited by *Verlag am Goetheanum*) of interviews given by the author during two conferences directed by Felix Schultz, Johann-Michael Ginther and Thomas Wehkamp at the *Freie Akademie* at Sammatz, Germany: 'Science between super-nature and sub-nature. Ways to an etheric technology' (1 November 1991), and 'Handling etheric space' (13 November 1992). The initiative for publication in German was taken by Felix Schultz.

Temple Lodge Publishing
51 Queen Caroline Street
London W6 9QL

Published by Temple Lodge 1995

Originally published in German under the title *Entscheidungskampf im Ätherischen, Moralische und ätherische Technik, Apokalyptische Symptome* by Verlag am Goetheanum, Dornach, in 1994

© Verlag am Goetheanum 1994
This translation © Temple Lodge Publishing 1995

The moral right of the author has been asserted under the Copyright, Designs and Patents Act, 1988

All rights reserved. No part of this publication may be reproduced, stored in a retrieval system, or transmitted, in any form or by any means, electronic, mechanical, photocopying, recording or otherwise, without the prior permission of the publishers

A catalogue record for this book is available from the British Library

ISBN 0 904693 68 6

Cover: art by Fergus Anderson, design by S. Gulbekian
Typeset by DP Photosetting, Aylesbury, Bucks
Printed and bound in Great Britain by Cromwell Press Limited, Broughton Gifford, Wiltshire

Contents

Part One

THE BATTLE FOR THE ETHERIC REALM

1
A lie is a lie is a lie ...

What is different now in the etheric realm? Is the etheric particularly relevant for us today?

The first thing we notice is a degree of hardening that is coming about in the etheric realm. For example, people nowadays have a greater tendency to adopt stereotyped attitudes; views about anything and everything have become increasingly stereotyped during the course of this century. Examples of this are the increase of fundamentalism, or the growing one-sidedness of what is seen as scientific or unscientific. This is the kind of thing that shows how the movements of the ether body are becoming less flexible. It is of course not the shape of the ether body but its movement that can rigidify. Rigid movements are possible in the ether body, and this is what causes inflexibility in thinking. This seems to me to be the development of something Rudolf Steiner spoke about in 1922 in lectures to young people when he discussed the influx of the empty phrase into cultural life.[1] I feel that the empty, meaningless phrase has gained ground tremendously during the course of this century. So much is said and written nowadays that is almost entirely meaningless. Not only are words or sentences or even whole speeches meaningless, but entire books have been written that are utterly devoid of meaning, and so on.

Behind this development lies the fact that the battle for the etheric realm predicted by Steiner in 1907 is indeed being waged today: 'Round about 1933 people will begin to appear who possess clairvoyant capacities that develop quite naturally ... Christ will appear in an etheric form ... Round about 1933 there will be representatives of schools of black magic who will wrongly prophesy the coming of a physical Christ ...'[2] By speaking about an appearance of Christ in the etheric realm Steiner was of course referring not only to a religious but also to a scientific concept. Christ appears to individuals. He is also perceptible in the processes of the earth's ether body, which are beginning to function in a different way. At the same time we can also observe an increase in the struggle of ahrimanic powers to seize the etheric realm in which Christ really does live, with the aim, you could say, of imprisoning Him there.

In connection with the culmination of materialism in the nineteenth century Steiner spoke about 'death by spiritual suffocation', comparing this sacrifice with the 'sacrifice in the physical world that took place in the Mystery of Golgotha'. He described this new event as a 'second crucifixion of Christ in the etheric realm'. 'This death by spiritual suffocation ... is a repetition of the Mystery of Golgotha in the realm that lies immediately behind our own, so that the awareness of Christ that was formerly hidden can be reborn in human souls on earth. This reborn awareness will become the clairvoyant perception of humanity in the twentieth century.'[3] As I see it, it is in this connection that Ahriman is endeavouring to curtail the flexibility of etheric movement.

What are the means by which Ahriman is endeavouring to harden the etheric realm?

There are two aspects to be considered: *repetition* (in connection with the etheric) and *truth*.

There is a close connection between the etheric realm and truth, since our thoughts can either be true or else mere models of things without any inner truth. During the course of the twentieth century Ahriman has convinced scientists that truth cannot be discovered by science: we can discover models which are more or less useful, but never the truth. The tragedy of Sir Karl R. Popper is one example. This British scientific philosopher of Austrian extraction (born in Vienna in 1902) believed passionately in the truth, but never succeeded in discovering it. At least, however, he believed in it, whereas other philosophers in this century don't even believe in it. Ahriman has thus succeeded—even through Popper!—in convincing scientists that truth cannot be found. As far as truth is concerned it seems we live with ideas of a kind of infinity, an infinity we never attain. Thus truth is something unattainable and asymptotic. This is an aspect Ahriman uses in order to fetter science, keeping it away from the truth in the way he works in the etheric realm.

The other aspect of Ahriman's work indicated above has to do with the way he can cause movement to petrify. In the etheric realm repetition can be a constructive force if it is not mere repetition but rather a rhythmical recurrence that is not an exact replication. We go to bed night after night—that is a rhythm—but we are never exactly the same person twice. Such repetition is rhythmical and alive, it is what we might call Christian rhythm. Ahriman, however, wants repetition to be mechanical and robotic, thus endeavouring to turn living human beings into robots through mechanical repetition. Alienation like this squeezes out the soul, and something that has been squeezed out can be seized upon by other powers.

On the one hand there is the battle for the etheric realm: Christ appears in the etheric realm where Ahriman is trying to drag everything down into material substance. On the other hand, though, countering Ahriman's endeavours, are the efforts to heal the etheric realm—efforts to mend today's ecological catastrophe and the suffering this is causing the elemental beings.

This throws light on the astonishing fact that anthroposophy works in a manner that is not immediately obvious.

The ecological catastrophe everyone is rightly talking about has, to some degree, been averted; it could have been far worse if an unprecedented awareness of ecological themes had not come about over the last 20 or 30 years. I remember when the paper *A Blueprint for Survival* appeared in Britain.[4] I was still quite young, and this paper was for me the first incisive indication that all was by no means well with our environment and that we were polluting and ruining it and using up the earth's mineral resources. Over the last 20 or 30 years this and many subsequent publications and actions by motivated individuals have helped generate environmental awareness.

Within the anthroposophical movement, however, this awareness had been sparked decades earlier by Steiner, and practical consequences were being drawn worldwide in biodynamic agriculture and so on. A little while ago at the London 'Festival for Mind, Body and Spirit' I heard a lecture by Peter Caddy who had had a lot to do with Findhorn. I gave a talk at the Festival too, which he attended. In his lecture he then said that developments leading up to the present crisis could have taken an entirely different course if people had listened to what Steiner had been saying many decades ago. It's all very well for anthroposophists to say such things, but when other contemporaries make these points they are more likely to attract public interest.

Anthroposophy is at work and brings about many things, but we have to realize that it doesn't make a great splash with what it does. Let us be content to work and offer the results of our work to the Time Spirit, Michael, and the Hierarchies, and leave it to the spiritual world to do whatever it wishes with them. Fame and recognition will not fall to us; and this surely is a truly Christian way of working. We work with anthroposophy. For example we watch the environmental movement gaining strength and influence as awareness of environmental problems reaches ever wider circles while we, who might be called the pioneers of this movement, remain more or less unknown. Yet the work of anthroposophists contributes to this progress, which is helped along by our understanding and meditation as general awareness grows. Without the efforts made by anthroposophists the scale of environmental destruction would have been worse.

It appears strange at first that every problem—whether ecological or even political—shows itself in the physical world; it is in the physical world that trees die. But then we begin to sense that many causes and possibilities for change are to be found in the etheric realm and not in the physical world. Christ appears in the etheric realm, Michael reaches out to us—from the etheric realm.

What can we do? Can we act in the etheric realm? How? Can we act in the physical world in a manner that affects the etheric realm?

Obviously we can't go about preaching anthroposophy, although we should do our best to make it known in the world. But this is not enough. Trusting that in truth every individual possesses an ether body, an astral body and an ego, even though he or she cannot or will not admit to this, we can endeavour to work with anthroposophy. Then we shall evoke a response in souls, a response that emanates from reality even if we can detect no external echo, or only a very small one. It is pointless to announce that people ought to accept or believe in anthroposophy. There is no such thing as 'ought'. No one, quite rightly, wants to feel they ought to believe in anthroposophy. On the other hand, in so far as anthroposophy is true and really describes spiritual facts, there are things that can be said to people who want to hear them because something connected with these things does live in their souls.

There need be no problem in this; a pupil of Michael only needs to hear or read something, and an awakening takes place within. Whether this individual then finds a way to the Anthroposophical Society or becomes a member of it is another question. Also, obstacles can arise even when a positive echo is aroused in a person, and then what is awakened immediately becomes submerged once more.

There is a real skill involved in finding out and hitting on an appropriate approach.

For example, telling someone about their own profession is least likely to be successful. Scientists know science very well, and teachers know how to teach, or musicians how to make music. If you try to tell musicians strange things about music, they won't want to listen. But if you tell musicians strange things about education, they will listen because in that field they are still open-minded; it is a field that has not yet been killed off for them. While I was studying engineering one of our professors used to stride up and down lecturing for three quarters of an hour and finish by saying: 'Well, that's killed that one off!' And he was quite right; that was exactly what he had done. This is not something that only used to happen in the past. It still goes on in schools and professional courses and universities: knowledge that has to be taught and learnt is first killed off for them, and this is thought to make it truly comprehensible. When a living idea from anthroposophy is then brought into the picture it is immediately rejected. But in a different field, one in which things have not yet been killed off for people, they remain open to what comes towards them. Perhaps not in every case, but certainly in most it is best to approach people with something that does not impinge on their immediate specialization.

This applies to individuals or groups, but considering the human race as a whole we have to search for a far wider angle of approach. We have to take into account the need to formulate anthroposophy in normal language. Speaking to politicians won't get us very far if we talk about 'ether body, astral body and ego'. But we might ask: What motivates people? Why do some people react to certain political opinions and not others? There is a great deal that can be said about motivation from the anthroposophical point of view using perfectly ordinary language.

The same kind of question can be asked of artists. Many artists lose their powers of imagination after a while, and they will be interested to hear something about how they might find a new source of imaginative inspiration. They will derive real help from this. People won't listen if we tell them about spiritual beings on the moon. The best point at which to begin is where they have concrete needs. In fact, we ought to lay far more emphasis on what the world needs than on what we want to give to the world.

What are the tools with which we can work in the etheric realm?

In the first place we discover suitable tools by following the path of spiritual science and practising meditation. This is the most effective thing we can do. The other thing is to think the truth with constancy and care in so far as we recognize it. This is especially effective in the etheric realm because that is where Ahriman is endeavouring to generate lies and untruths. When we make a genuine effort to work with truth we are also working with the etheric. Of course the same also goes for what we try to do in meditation. For example, if we meditate daily in a certain rhythm we are working with the etheric realm and causing something to happen in it. We can meditate for our own development, but we can also meditate not for ourselves but for the evolution of the world. This is an exceedingly important tool. It is at once the most obvious and the most fundamental.

What does it mean to lie?

It is easy to forget what a lie is, for lies can be used in such a calculated fashion that even their perpetrators regard them as the truth. In esoteric life, however, great strictness is in force in this matter. A lie is a lie is a lie! Even if someone is dying and we fail to tell him or her the truth when asked, we are telling a lie, esoterically speaking. In every case we have to decide whether to burden ourselves with the karma this generates.

It is quite difficult to imagine ourselves in the etheric realm. Is there a bridge that can help us find the way to doing so?

Obviously a genuine experience of the etheric realm only comes about when we actually enter it. But can we arrive at a concept of it before this happens?

We can indeed, for example through the very helpful insights to be gained from projective geometry, and within this especially the concept of counter-space as understood by George Adams and Louis Locher-Ernst, and then by Olive Whicher and Lawrence Edwards and others.[5] All these people worked very hard on this for decades.

The first thing that happens when we cross the threshold from the sense-perceptible into the supersensible world, i.e. initially into the etheric realm, is that our consciousness is turned inside out.[6] This is the first step we take, not the last. Therefore in our geometric and scientific research our preparatory work is concerned with the concepts of polarity and inversion. In conversation Rudolf Steiner used to demonstrate what he was trying to describe by borrowing a glove from one of his listeners and turning it inside out. For a start this image of the glove turned inside out is sufficient, but after a while it ceases to help us further.

The next step is to think of our ordinary consciousness as being in a centre from which we can look outwards in all directions, imagining infinity as being infinitely far away.

Then we think of ourselves as being at infinity, and as a result we no longer experience it as infinite. We live with our consciousness in the circumference and look inwards towards the centre, unreachably far inwards towards the centre. That is where, looking back having crossed the threshold, we discover the physical body. We look down at our body; we look from the circumference, from the outside into something, and then we feel that the sun is our heart, Jupiter our liver, and so on.[7] We look into these with a consciousness that is spread out all around us. There, infinitely far inwards, in every direction, lies infinity. We have now arrived at a consciousness that resembles very closely that of the etheric realm. When we achieve a consciousness of this kind and have this experience together, we find ourselves, you might say, together in the etheric realm sharing the same circumference. The difference between us would be that one physical body is here, another there. Almost everything would be shared; we share the sun as a heart, we share a liver. There would be vastly more that we share than that separates us. The only difference would be in one single, minute and yet very important aspect: our own, particular infinity. One individual's infinity is different from that of another. But here, in the physical world, we all have the same shared infinity. This is a small indication of how very radically we have to describe a turning inside out or a polarity when we are speaking about counter-space. It is a 'space' such as that found inside the sun, which is why it is also termed 'sun-space'.

2
Return to chaos—etheric technology

Research into etheric technology: attempts to build the 'Strader machine'.[8] Are there moral objections to this in view of Rudolf Steiner's statement that an entirely selfless arrangement of society would have to exist before work could be done to develop a technology based on harmonized vibrations?[9] Surely the present state of affairs is a long way from that selfless social order!

Because of this statement I have for many years left on one side the question of etheric technology, and in particular the Strader machine. Although I found it exceedingly interesting I thought that we ought not to occupy ourselves with it at all. This attitude has only begun to change in the last three or four years since questions raised by other researchers have begun to generate in me a sense that perhaps I ought to take up this work again. This is how things happen in life. The spiritual world speaks to us first and foremost through other individuals rather than out of nothingness. It speaks to us through other people and their questions regarding the requirements of life.

I still feel that there is no point in trying to build a Strader machine, and anyway such a machine would only function for Strader himself. The whole subject is probably one of those open secrets in the Goethean sense, a riddle we shall only solve once we have learnt to build all kinds of machines, ones like the Strader machine as well as quite different ones. I do, however, see the sense in really seeking to come to grips with the principles that would govern the functioning of such a machine. It could even be right to build a working model, but not in order to present it in public or take out a patent. Anyway it would be pointless to patent it since it would only work for its inventor! Machines like the Strader machine or the Keely motor only work when their inventors operate them.

One thing is important, though. Somebody is sure to stumble across this secret hinted at by Steiner. In America, for example, there are groups doing a lot of research in a field known as 'psychotronics'. They assume that electromagnetic waves and similar phenomena affect the human psyche and can influence our state of consciousness. They work with quantum physics, with what goes on in a vacuum, and so on. People are trying to come to grips with the energy of the vacuum. In fact, there is justification for understanding the energy of the vacuum as etheric vibration. We cannot ignore the possibility that people might succeed in grasping this, although from the point of view of quantum physics this does not appear likely at the moment. But because the possibility exists—and I feel very strongly that sooner or later people will stumble across this secret—it is very important that we should have a sufficient grasp of what is involved so that we can understand the way these forces work.

If our karma presents us with the opportunity—and I'm convinced that we shall experience such opportunities—we ought to make sure we understand things; we ought to be in a position to recognize such a thing if it has come or will come into being. If we know what it is all about, the secret brotherhoods won't be able to do much with what they discover. But they would be able to make a great deal of use of something that remained a mystery and about which we knew nothing. Our strength as anthroposophists does not lie in being able to make huge amounts of money or put together armies; our strength lies in our knowledge. Especially in this field of the etheric realm we ought to be armed with knowledge.

Is it sufficient to know, or is it necessary to publish such knowledge?

The knowledge itself is enough. Whether to talk about it or not—this is something that raises many questions, and a satisfactory answer can only be got in an actual situation. If, for example, someone were to give a lecture about it, or write an article in a daily newspaper saying that this kind of machine had been developed, a *perpetuum mobile*, most probably the speaker or writer would be believed by hardly anyone. Whatever the hype accompanying it, it would not be given credence.

The essential thing is to know. In a specific case it might then be appropriate to say something, or even to construct the model of a machine, but this is pure conjecture at the moment. The first step is to know, the second to recognize, and the third then depends on the actual situation.

Are there concrete signs indicating that research is being done into a kind of materialistic etheric technology?

It is difficult in these fields to differentiate between the crazy ones and the idealists on the one hand and the serious researchers on the other. Who checks out the statements made by people like Bearden and others who have said and written quite extraordinary things (for example about the sinking of the submarine *Thresher* by 'occult forces')? Who knows, perhaps they're right. How do you verify something like that? An immense maelstrom of pseudo-mystical views surrounds such things, dragging them down into the abyss, so it's extraordinarily difficult to distinguish between truth and invention. People who give lectures about these things without even understanding the basic physics that applies to what they are saying are not rare. For example, they discern a total correspondence between two fields where in fact there is no such thing. They are particularly sure they have understood the Theory of Relativity when actually they haven't the faintest idea of what it's about. They may take their departure from what they think is a symmetry between the electron and the photon. But they are wrong, and yet they draw far-reaching conclusions from it. A great deal of nonsense is talked, especially in these fields.

If you read an article about them in a journal there is a 90 per cent chance that it will be wrong. Any specialist reading a newspaper article on a subject well known to him or her will soon discover that at least half the facts are wrong, even with something as simple as a new road bridge. It appears to be quite impossible to present facts correctly; it's quite astounding. If you try to gather information about what is going on in Russia, or the former Yugoslavia, you're in trouble because it's pointless to believe what appears in newspapers or on television. The little square box gives the impression that the whole of Northern Ireland is living in a state of war, and yet the scene shown is taking place in some tiny corner of a district of Belfast. This can be very confusing.

However, the positive thing about the media is that they can heighten our awareness of the existence of a distant location and of the people who live there. The media give us an awareness of these things that in my opinion is strong enough to make it possible for people here to forge links with those in Bosnia, in Russia or Ireland while they are asleep. A few days later you then wake up with a sense for what is really happening. This sense can be trained, so that you begin to see through the bewildering tendencies in the media and gain a feeling for what is actually going on. Initially you can't explain what generates this feeling. But from the anthroposophical point of view you can explain this awareness through knowing that the Angels of the people here form links with the Angels of those over there through which they create a sense for what is going on in those people, a sense for what is really going on behind the scenes. The same applies with regard to anything we encounter in connection with etheric technology. Here, too, in sleep, we can develop a sense for what is true and real. If we are sufficiently awake and actively search for it we can also discover where this spiritual link shows itself in our waking life as well.

For example: chaos research ...

Chaos research is a relevant field, and there is also a lot going on in others, such as that of 'psychotronics' already mentioned. One wonders why so much is being invested in chaos research. One of the reasons may be that there are problems too complex for ordinary mathematics. A simple example of this is the weather. Chaos theory provides a starting point that might make it possible to investigate the processes that are behind meteorological phenomena. That can be one of the reasons for promoting chaos research. Large firms such as IBM and others are carrying out extensive research projects in this field. A great deal of research has indeed been done. How many people have already drawn Mandelbrot-Sets in bright colours on their computer monitors? The point is, however, that it becomes possible in the mechanical field to achieve very large effects from very tiny influences, to the extent that a mechanistic world, a pre-determined world in the sense of Laplace, turns out to be exceptional. Chaos theory shows that the existence of such a world is extremely unlikely. And yet within it a kind of self-regulation takes place. In the sense of Darwin's theory of evolution the Laplace element has, you might say, taken pride of place in our consciousness. This is what we first meet in science. It has taken a while to discover that possibly, instead, a chaotic world lies behind everything. If we really do discover that chaos is the norm in the physical world, then it will be understood that the physical world will be as solid, as un-chaotic, as sclerotic as it is now only for about another 12 thousand years, which is the span of time needed for human freedom to evolve. After that chaos will take the upper hand. The question, of course, will be whether this chaos is creative or destructive.

Presumably there are also other motives for this research, but it is scarcely possible to find out what they are. Obviously IBM and the other firms give good reasons. Why certain researchers receive funds for specific projects while others don't is an occult field of research in its own right—and an extremely interesting one, because it shows what influences are active behind the scenes that steer the intentions of human beings. Such influences are especially active in people's instincts. Many a researcher, when asked why he took on this project and rejected that one, is incapable of giving a sensible reason because he has simply sensed instinctively that one seems right and the other wrong.

I remember a meeting on one of the top floors of a New York skyscraper. We were a group of people who had to decide whether several million dollars were to be spent on a certain project. There we sat at the top of a New York skyscraper having dinner and looking out over the sea of lights below. It was quite cosy. The conversation roamed back and forth; we had no diagrams showing ideas on one side and value assessments on the other, as might be imagined when a funding body works at coming to a decision. What we did could be described as tasting our way towards the outcome, entirely instinctively, until suddenly we said: 'Yes, that's it!' This is something that happens very often.

What is expressed in such instincts? Who checks them? People don't know why their instinctive feeling about something runs this way and not that—at least not until they have set out on the path of self-knowledge. That is why I think that research especially in the field of etheric technology promises a great deal.[10] It will create a sense and an understanding for such machines. I'm sure of this. That is the 'good reason' why such research should be generously funded.

3

Rupert Sheldrake: 'theosophical' and 'anthroposophical' ether

Rupert Sheldrake is a well-known scientist; when a new book by him is published it attracts a great deal of media attention and discussion. His views on the end of materialism, for example, or the learning processes in nature, and so on, are astonishing.[11]

In many ways these are promising signs. Sheldrake has reached an idea that ought to be accepted as scientific in accordance with the usual guidelines. But it's very interesting to see how mainstream scientists react. They don't like it; they don't like it one bit! Although the *New Scientist*, for example, gave him strong support, *Nature* said the best thing that could be done would be to burn his books. The Establishment doesn't like having its own methods adopted and then used against it, but this is exactly what Sheldrake has done. As a qualified scientist and researcher he has established a hypothesis that anyone can check. Everyone has to admit that this hypothesis can be checked in accordance with the usual guidelines. But competent scientists are offended. They feel thoroughly uncomfortable and fear there is something mystical about it.

At a meeting in London we asked Sheldrake whether he thought that his morphogenetic fields might have anything to do with the ether body. He answered in the negative, probably for a quite specific reason. He was referring to something that I call the theosophical concept of the etheric, which differs considerably from that of anthroposophy.[12] Sheldrake is a theosophist, or at least he is a member of the

Theosophical Society. He shrinks from a confusion of his morphogenetic fields with the etheric, but his assumption is that we mean the theosophical concept with which he is familiar. He doesn't want his fields to be confused with this. If he really understood the anthroposophical concept of the etheric he might be more likely to see a connection.

He is concerned that his hypothesis should remain in the scientific realm and does not want any mystical jargon, as it would then be termed, to be linked with his research. This has to be respected. I regard it as a sensible way of proceeding, since it opens the way ahead for further developments. I find the fundamental idea in his first book extremely interesting although the way he develops it appears to me to be very materialistic. Surprisingly, his mode of thinking is totally inadequate, and this is a difficulty that cannot be overlooked.

His concept of morphogenetic fields is without doubt broad enough to encompass, as I see it, the astral rather than the etheric realm in certain aspects, especially in the parts that have a temporal character. In this connection we can consider Steiner's remark that the astral aspect rays into us from the time prior to birth.[13] This indication is in a way an exact image of what Sheldrake is talking about. Something from the past rays into the present and influences it. Steiner anticipated this discovery by many years. But he used concepts that scientists at the time couldn't relate to, and this is still the case today. Sheldrake is trying to ensure that his idea avoids having any concepts inflicted on it, since this would all too easily provide a pretext for judgements like *Nature*'s recommendation to burn such publications.

I think it is extremely commendable to set up a hypothesis that can be checked and yet obviously doesn't fit into any current paradigm.

The next step now would be to go beyond his materialistic idea of fields! However, I believe this will only be possible once the concept of counter-space as already

described achieves recognition. A group of anthroposophists in Britain is putting all its energies into bringing
this about. It ought to be possible. Academic mathemati-
cians who, as we have seen, find it particularly difficult to
accept new ideas in their field must surely admit, if they are
familiar with projective geometry, that it does possess this
built-in polarity. They can arrive at it either via the point or
via the plane. Surely this is unavoidable. It is quite simply a
given, what Whitehead called a 'stubborn, irreducible fact'.
We are confident that eventually we shall achieve recognition of the correctness of these results, for example
through the work of Lawrence Edwards or parallel research
on the obvious cosmic influences on the plant world.
Recognition of this other side of geometry would then
contribute a great deal to a better understanding of what
Sheldrake is talking about—a better understanding, perhaps, than he himself has.

4
Radioactivity: when the real challenge will come

Basing his statement on memoirs by Ludwig Polzer-Hoditz, Ehrenfried Pfeiffer once stated in a lecture that radioactivity had only existed in its present form since the Mystery of Golgotha.[14]

In my opinion this statement is based on a misunderstanding. I have also discussed this problem with Georg Unger.[15] There is a passage in which Rudolf Steiner was endeavouring to explain to a lay public what 'half-life' meant—and we have to remember that these things were quite new at the time. Nowadays almost everyone knows what is meant by 'half-life', but at that time hardly anyone did: 'People talk about the characteristics of radium … Today people know that the radium present on the earth's surface prior to the year AD 140 has now dissipated, that it is no longer radium. The radium present today only came into being after the year AD 140 …'[16] Here we see Steiner mentioning a specific date as an example, a date not far removed from that of the Mystery of Golgotha: 'The radium present today only came into being after the year AD 140.' Some of the audience, hearing this, thought he meant that radioactivity as such has only been in existence since the Mystery of Golgotha! These people failed to take into account other indications by Steiner to the effect that radioactivity came into being in the middle of the Atlantean period, i.e. at the middle point of earth evolution.[17]

The point of time indicated there is more likely to be the correct one. Up to that time the earth was in an upward mode of evolution, whereas from then onwards the physical earth began the decline that eventually will end in its complete disintegration. Radioactivity thus marks the beginning of the dissolution of the earth, or, to put it another way, of the re-spiritualization of the earth. I think the proper interpretation would be to say that radioactivity did not begin with the Mystery of Golgotha but that through the Mystery of Golgotha Christ penetrated so deeply into matter that he brought this already existing characteristic of matter into the sphere of influence of the etheric realm.

The most important thing for us to do is to link ourselves with Christ in the etheric realm. This is the most important thing we can do. The etheric realm received an inexhaustibly powerful force through the Christ impulse. A more general image of etheric power is the way a tiny seedling can break through concrete. So I'm convinced that an ether body steeped in Christ is almost certainly capable of withstanding radioactivity. Even in the case of nuclear war I feel sure there would be some souls strong enough to overcome the radioactivity with their ether bodies.

When Christ penetrated into the earth's substance at the Mystery of Golgotha, this substance already contained the capacity for radioactivity. I don't believe that the radioactivity of matter was brought about by Christ but I do think that the possibility for this radioactivity to be healed was given by Him.

In this context it's worth remembering that a luciferic inclination is also possible in our relationship with the physical world, namely, the tendency to steer clear of it. There are so many people who don't want anything to do with the material world, who don't want to be weighed down by matter! And there is also an ahrimanic inclination: to enter too deeply into it. Between these two there always stands the Christ impulse, the impulse to lead those who want to keep away from it down into it, and the impulse to help those who have become too deeply enmeshed to find their way out of it again. In both cases it is the impulse to maintain the balance between the two inclinations.

Is it necessary today to use nuclear power in some way as a source of energy simply because it exists and something has to be done with it? It is tempting to answer this question in the negative.

Many people feel they ought to say No. For my part I find this a theoretical question since we already have in store so much nuclear waste with a half-life of millions of years that we have simply got to cope with the problem whatever happens, even in the unlikely event that as of this moment the construction and use of nuclear power stations were to be outlawed. I am convinced that as evolution proceeds we shall have to be strong enough to handle ever more dangerous forces. We shall not make progress in our evolution if we try to avoid dealing with dangerous forces. Fundamentally the attitude that says, 'We want nothing to do with radioactivity,' is rather a luciferic one. It's an attitude of sweeping the problem under the carpet.

Since we have to come out on top in our battle with nuclear power we must do so on the basis of knowledge, knowledge that is not abstract. In a sense this has not happened with regard to nuclear power as it exists at present. We are dealing with the problem of nuclear waste and so forth on the basis of abstract ideas, since we don't know what the effects of background radiation are and so on. The measures that have been taken, and everything that has been initiated in this connection, have been done without any conception of what the final effects might be. We possess no knowledge in the sense of a 'moral technique' as described in *The Philosophy of Spiritual Activity*.[18] Moral technique implies a full understanding of all the implications before taking any action. This has not been the case in the way the problem of nuclear power has been handled hitherto. However, merely to talk of 'altars of Satan' while warning against any involvement with nuclear power is also nothing more than a luciferic enchantment! I do agree, though, that nuclear power received a strong ahrimanic thrust too early on.

Is atomic energy connected with luciferic powers because it works through destroying physical substance?

Atomic energy is really ahrimanic in so far as it has to do with the freeing of the forces within the atom. Naturally this is only a tiny beginning if we are thinking of transforming matter into energy, which has not happened yet! To my knowledge no more than one or two atoms have so far been destroyed. If a cubic centimetre of salt were to be transformed into energy in the sense of Einstein's equation it would keep an electric cooker going for two million years or longer—that is how much energy lies hidden in a cubic centimetre of salt. So we can't talk of having succeeded yet in transforming matter into energy. What has been achieved, however, is the freeing of nuclear binding energy. But this hardly amounts to a genuine transformation. So what we at present understand to be nuclear power is mere child's-play compared with what is still to come when we have really found out how to transform matter itself. That's when the real challenge will come.

Part Two

CONTEMPORARY EVENTS ILLUMINED BY THE BOOK OF REVELATION

1
Symptoms of the Apocalypse today

*How can anthroposophy build a bridge between contemporary
phenomena and ancient prophecies such as the Apocalypse of St
John?*[19]

We must assume that the Book of Revelation—although as a
document it is nearly two thousand years old—is still valid
today. It describes a reality: images of an initiation, a Jewish
initiation against an obviously Christian background. This
initiation document is especially important, as Rudolf
Steiner pointed out a number of times, because today
mankind as a whole is crossing the threshold.

What is meant by this? Whether we cross the threshold to
the spiritual world as individuals, in consequence of our
personal work on the esoteric path, or whether we do so
through a natural, inborn faculty, events await us in the
spiritual world that resemble those described in the Book of
Revelation. Our experiences may not necessarily be exactly
as those described there, for the imaginative pictures in the
Book of Revelation are those of the Christian-Jewish initiate
John. The pictures we experience today may be different,
but their dramatic content remains. It is the inner, dramatic
content that we see, not the pictures that perhaps differ—in
the manner described by Steiner in connection with dreams.
In imaginative knowledge we have to take note of the
dramatic relationships between the images. And this drama
is the same now as in the Book of Revelation.

This is the case for those who cross the threshold indi-
vidually, and to a certain extent also when humanity as a

whole crosses the threshold. The drama of the images in the Apocalypse is just beginning in our time to have a particular significance, and I mean this in the scientific sense. However, it has also been possible for some time to observe a trend towards apocalyptic 'visions', and this should be regarded more as an expression of sensationalism.

The following is what is now happening. Rudolf Steiner pointed to the human instincts as being on the increase and growing more and more inclined to irrupt into social life where they cause ever greater chaos if anthroposophy fails to become effective as a cultural impulse. Their destructive traits arise from the fact that our human capacity to think contains a powerfully destructive force which is necessary because our sharply differentiating consciousness is founded on processes of death which are active in our subconscious.[20]

As we begin to push forward into the etheric realm with our consciousness we unleash these instincts; it really is a kind of unleashing. Consciousness passes through four stages into the ether body: through the warmth ether, the light ether, the sound or chemical ether, and the life ether. Intensified thinking can proceed across these four stages, each time unleashing the corresponding instincts.

Anthroposophists tend to depict reality in diagrams and I've always tried to be careful about this. These insights, however, have not arisen out of a diagram but out of experience.

I have noticed that there are instincts which initially appear to be utterly chaotic. Their source can be discovered to be the warmth ether, since, as an ether, warmth has a chaotic effect which also means that it has a positive, liberating and productive power. Obviously such a power can also take on destructive characteristics. Our most essential inner nature is related to warmth, and we take hold of our physical body through it. The ego is developed precisely through overcoming chaos. If instead these chaotic instincts irrupt here, then we lose our humanity, becoming like beasts.

Proceeding further, now into the realm of the light ether—light and darkness—we also find chaotic instincts, but here with more of a religious character. Fundamentalism, for example, bears the stamp of such instincts. What is fundamentalism? When am I behaving in a fundamentalist manner? When I want to be absolutely clear about things, and whether I am seeing them in the right or the wrong way, and when I am then absolutely convinced that I am right and everyone else wrong, then I am behaving in a fundamentalist manner. Fundamentalism provides us with absolute inner psychological certainty. It is a question of light and dark. Fundamentalism makes its appearance when we enter (unconsciously) into the realm of the light ether.

This process can be related to the second horseman of the Apocalypse, the one who stands for the (Persian) cultural era of light and darkness.[21] Fundamentalism today is a powerful and effective force, and the power with which these instincts break loose is alarming. It becomes very clear that fundamentalism is no theory, for it lives far more deep down in human beings, namely, in their instincts.

Instincts of quite a different kind motivate people in high political situations or in elevated positions in the world of finance. I have already described the instinctive manner in which these people work. They do indeed have a kind of instinct for what they have to do. In the *New Scientist* the following question was the subject of an editorial in 1992: What is the matter with economic science?! People trained in this discipline have the most contradictory views and opinions! We might perhaps try to explain this by saying that economic science is a very young science. However, this explanation is inadequate. In fact many leading economists take no account at all of this science, since they make their decisions on the basis of their sure instincts. The question is, of course, whether these instincts are social or antisocial. In most cases the consequences are antisocial. People have an instinctive sense for figures and proportions. These instincts are related to the chemical (or sound) ether. For example, it is quite easy to discern a feeling for rhythms in the financial markets of the great metropolitan centres.

When we come finally to the life ether we have to do with the individuality—or its opposite. The world-wide irruption of nationalism must be seen as a perversion in this realm. The fourth horseman of the Apocalypse can help us understand this. He stands for the Graeco-Roman era in which, in contrast to earlier cultural eras, individual intelligence, the personal capacity to think, became effective for the first time. Thinking, and also death, are connected with this horseman. The positive aspect is the individuality, while the negative side can be described as follows. When a Roman said, 'I am a Roman *citizen*,' he meant himself as an individual. But if he stressed that he was a *Roman* citizen he was more concerned with his Roman aspect. (The Greeks were still inclined to experience themselves as Athenians or Spartans rather than individuals.) Today it remains relevant to ask English or German or French people what aspect of themselves they consider to be salient. You can do this research on yourself as well as on others.

What are the positive powers we might train within ourselves in order to counter these instincts?

The first step is to confront them inwardly. We know that the anthroposophical schooling path is not a bed of roses. It forces us to confront these unsavoury aspects.

As a second step we need to develop positive powers within ourselves in order to stand firm in this confrontation and have something positive with which to confront these instincts. Steiner recommended that we train four specific feelings which should accompany the way we develop our thinking if we want to experience reality. It isn't a purely intellectual matter, and it's interesting to see how things come together here.

The first feeling Steiner mentioned in this connection is that of awe, of wonderment, which can become the faculty with which the correct starting point is perceived.[22] Intellectually I can't decide where I ought to begin. There are a thousand possibilities. Which one should I choose? A feeling of wonderment guides me in the end to the point where my karma wants to lead me and to the questions that are truly my concern—provided that my wonderment is genuine and founded on humility. Through genuine wonderment I find my way to the starting point that is the karmically correct one for my path.

The second feeling to be developed is that of reverence. By faithfully following the path of wonderment I soon arrive at the door of reverence. Without reverence I remain a sanguine, wondering first at one thing and then at another. My wonderment remains superficial. With this second feeling, if it fills my thinking, I can consistently follow the real direction of my research.

A third feeling then has to be added so that I don't forever follow my path while practising wonderment and reverence until I lose the world and find myself alone. In order to remain properly connected to reality in my search I need a third feeling which must permeate my thinking: 'the feeling of being in wisdom-filled harmony with the universal laws'.

The fourth feeling to be developed has a strong character of will. It involves the realization that I must give up my own opinions and favourite ideas. I must be capable of giving these up—together with my own lower self. Only then shall I be able to attain reality. 'Surrendering oneself to the course of world evolution' is what Steiner called this fourth condition of soul, in which I place myself into the evolution of the world through a free deed as one who shares in the responsibility for it.[23] If this step is not taken reality remains just out of reach, hidden behind a veil of my own opinions, prejudices and interests.

By developing these four feelings and by practising these four powers here on the earth we bring them within reach of others in our civilization. They thus become cultural impulses.

2
Science at the threshold

Individual people as well as humankind as a whole have reached the threshold to the spiritual world or indeed have already crossed it. This crossing of the threshold can be observed in physics and science in general. Reading certain publications as a non-scientist one can easily be irritated by many items that appear to be unreliable, but there are also others that are very significant. What is meant by saying that science is at the threshold?

The first point to be clear about is that science has been at the threshold since the beginning of the twentieth century, as shown by a number of characteristic aspects appearing at the turn of the century, and more especially in the mid-1920s. At that time it was immensely difficult for scientists to understand the idea of 'matter' at all. In the nineteenth century people thought they knew what they meant by 'matter', but then it suddenly became unbelievably difficult. They discovered that matter was governed by some rather extraordinary laws which differed considerably from the laws pertaining to motor cars or coffee cups, and so on— such as the laws of the electron, the theory of electrons. For example, it is impossible to find the exact location of an electron while at the same time knowing how fast it is travelling. This is a world quite different from the one with which we are familiar. If I want to catch a bus I have to know simultaneously both where it is and how fast it is moving! But this is not a law that holds good in the world of sub-atomic physics.

Even Einstein said in the 1920s that one felt as though the

rug had been pulled from under one's feet. Steiner, too, frequently stressed that we lose the solid ground under our feet when approaching the threshold. Physicists in the 1920s experienced this very strongly indeed. They lost the firm ground under their feet. They no longer had the idea that matter was something solid, which would have been rather a reassuring idea for a materialist to have. Many sensed this very strongly. Wolfgang Pauli (1900–58), for example, said that physics had got itself into a terrible muddle and he would greatly prefer to be working as a comedian! We sense the proximity of the threshold through such statements.

Another aspect of this whole problem is that different laws pertain on this side than on the other side of the threshold. On this side we have firm ground under our feet, but as we approach the threshold we have to learn to live in two worlds at once, and no longer only in the physical, sense-perceptible one. We have to learn to take account at the same time of the laws of the spiritual world, and these are different.[24] Physicists have no choice and they don't know how to get out of this predicament. Working in their chosen discipline they notice that quite other laws pertain.

This brings us to a second characteristic of the proximity of the threshold that became ever more noticeable during the 1920s and 1930s. It is the element of fear that engulfs us as we approach the threshold. In many people this came to be expressed as a fear of technology as such. They felt that its apocalyptic character was leading to ever greater difficulties, ever new dangers, ever increasing toxicity, and so on. We must of course ask ourselves whether it is technology itself that is conjuring up all these apocalyptic threats, or is it the people who apply the technology? Whatever the answer, this fear exists, and I look on it as a further aspect of the threshold with regard to science.

A third aspect was described by Steiner in his lectures *Boundaries of Natural Science*,[25] in which he stated that within the sense-perceptible world we encounter the world of phenomena. He said that Goethe had stopped when he reached the veil of phenomena; although he was searching for the archetypal phenomena, when he reached this threshold he did not try to step across. Physics today, however, dislikes this threshold. It would very much like to step across it and discover beyond it ever tinier particles— and the technology evolving for this is leading to the construction of ever larger machines. In 1918 Steiner pointed out that experiments in physics provide a basis for our consciousness as we push our way further and further behind the physical world.[26] But why are experiments necessary?

If we approach physical reality with a consciousness that has not been transformed we find that this reality sends us to sleep. It's not that our eyelids close; what happens is that we can no longer think. We attain a degree of consciousness and then get stuck. This is nature's way of protecting itself—and us. By carrying out experiments, however, we create conditions that allow us to stay awake without undergoing any spiritual development. To enter properly into the realm that lies beyond the threshold, and remain awake, or not be stunned, we would have to prepare ourselves for this supersensible realm by schooling our faculties. To cross the threshold without being Goethean scientists we need the help of a machine, and a gigantic one at that, such as CERN's particle accelerator at Meyrin near Geneva. These machines are so huge that they enable us to stay awake a very long way beyond the threshold. We need them if we want to observe the tiniest particles in a millionth of a second without falling asleep. On the other hand these machines demonstrate to us the significant scale of our spiritual work, for our path of schooling is capable of becoming a substitute for them. What an interesting view of the situation this presents! In this sense science has already gone a long way beyond the threshold.

Steiner gave a number of impressive descriptions of the way destructive forces come into play if the threshold is crossed without schooling.[27] Nuclear research as it is conducted today means that the danger of going astray is very close at hand. Scientists have crossed the threshold without adequate preparation; they have gained access to terribly destructive forces that are now in use, for example in nuclear bombs. Even when, with the best will in the world, the intention is to use such forces for peaceful purposes, their destructive potential and all the dangers this involves quite simply remains a threat.

Science achieves an immense input, but what kind of input is it? It is a question of how much strength we can muster, of how conscious we can be. The intense effort of remaining wide awake in every moment very soon makes us extremely tired, whereas there is no exertion involved in just 'having a nice time' and letting time flow by without noticing whether ten minutes or an hour has passed. To enter truly into the tiniest span of time demands enormous strength. This also has to do with Heisenberg's uncertainty principle, and Steiner spoke about this, too.[28] We are talking about the polarity between consciousness and life. When we have absolute clarity, total awareness, mathematical precision, we have no life; everything is dead. Or we have vitality in the world of our ideas, but little clarity. We have to find our path while taking this polarity into account, for we need both life and clarity. Progress involves attaining more and more of both of these. And yet the more we have of one at any particular moment, the less we have of the other. Engineers call this 'Sod's law': the more the one increases, the less we have of the other—unless we attain a higher level. Heisenberg's equation is a kind of reflection of this fact, stated in physical terms. The more we know about the energy in a process the less we can determine its moment in time. Or, vice versa, the more aware we are of the point in time when something takes place, the less we can say how much energy is involved. So the more precise we want to be the more energy we have to muster. Or, speaking anthroposophically, the more conscious we are at a particular point of time the greater is the amount of vitality we need to achieve this.

Scientists, therefore, are striving to cross the threshold without venturing inwards as whole human beings, down into their inmost heart, which is to be found beyond the threshold.

Yes, they step across the threshold with their intellect only, not as whole human beings. If they were to cross the threshold as whole human beings they would not be entering the kingdom of Ahriman. There is always a danger of crossing the threshold unprepared and, if we do, Ahriman will be waiting for us there, with a world he has created for us. If we are properly prepared we enter a different world, one in which we find the same things but seen from a Christian perspective.

Notes

1. See Steiner, R., *The Younger Generation, Educational and Spiritual Impulses for Life in the Twentieth Century* (GA 217), tr. R. M. Querido, New York: Anthroposophic Press 1984, lecture of 3 October 1922: 'With the vogue of the "cliché" there began to develop lack of thought, lack of sound sentiments, lack of will, which are now on the upgrade. These characteristics were the immediate outcome of the "empty phrase", the "cliché" ... Those who are sensitive to such matters are aware of the gradual entrance of what inevitably accompanies the "empty phrase" ... truth, as experienced inwardly by the soul, dies away...'
2. Steiner, R., *Esoteric Christianity and the Mission of Christian Rosenkreutz* (GA 130), tr. P. Wehrle, London: Rudolf Steiner Press 1984, lecture of 28 September 1911.
3. Steiner, R., *Christ at the Time of the Mystery of Golgotha and Christ in the Twentieth Century* (in GA 152), tr. D. S. Osmond, London: Rudolf Steiner Press 1966, lecture of 2 May 1913.
4. See 'A Blueprint for Survival', in *The Ecologist*, 2, No. 1, pp. 1–44, 1977. Also Carson, R., *Silent Spring*, New York: Crest 1964.
5. See Edwards, L., *The Field of Form*, Edinburgh: Floris Books 1982; Adams, G. & Whicher, O., *The Plant Between Sun and Earth*, London: Rudolf Steiner Press 1980; Adams, G., *Physical and Ethereal Spaces*, London: Rudolf Steiner Press 1965; Whicher, O., *Sun Space*, London: Rudolf Steiner Press 1989.
6. See Steiner, R., *Life Between Death and a New Birth as Image of the Future Jupiter Existence* (GA 208), tr. V. E. Watkin, Typescript Z340 in Rudolf Steiner Library, London, lecture of 21 October 1921.
7. See for example Steiner, R., *An Occult Physiology* (GA 128), tr. E. Frommer, London: Rudolf Steiner Press 1983, lecture of 28 March 1911; and Steiner, R., *True and False Paths in Spiritual*

Investigation (GA 243), tr. A. Parker, London: Rudolf Steiner Press 1986.

8. See *Beiträge zur Rudolf Steiner Gesamtausgabe*, Booklet 107, Dornach, Michaelmas 1991: 'Der Strader-Apparat' (The Strader Machine). This booklet contains a hitherto unpublished lecture by Rudolf Steiner, 'Geisteswissenschaft, Naturwissenschaft, Technik' (Spiritual Science, Natural Science, Technology). It also contains a chronological survey on 'mechanical occultism, the Keely motor, the future of technology as discussed in R. Steiner's lectures' as well as a bibliography of literature on these subjects.

9. See also Pfeiffer, E., *Notes and Lectures, Compendium 1*, Spring Valley/New York 1991: 'I once asked Rudolf Steiner when the proper time would come for the application of etheric forces in technology. He said this would be when the three-fold ordering of society had been achieved ...' (Quoted after Lievegoed, B., *The Battle for the Soul*, tr. P. Mees, Stroud: Hawthorn Press 1994.)

10. See Steiner, R., *The Karma of Untruthfulness*, Vol. I (GA 173), tr. J. Collis, London: Rudolf Steiner Press/New York: Anthroposophic Press, 1988, lecture of 18 December 1916: 'In the comparatively near future ... something will come into being ... which will enable people to make use of the delicate vibrations in their etheric bodies as a driving force with which to run machines. Machines will exist which are dependent on people and people will transfer their own vibrations to the machines. They alone will be capable of setting these machines in motion by means of certain vibrations stimulated by themselves.'

11. See Sheldrake, R., *A New Science of Life*, London: Blond & Briggs 1981.

12. This was also spoken of by the author in a lecture given in Hamburg on 30 October 1991 concerning 'A New Approach to the Four Ethers'. The distinction between the 'theosophical' and 'anthroposophical' concepts of the ether was characterized by the fact that the former approaches the ether and akasha as something ever finer, in an analogous way to seeing air as something finer than water, whereas the latter sees the ether as being *negative* in respect to the physical, not merely

'finer stuff'. It involves an inversion of our consciousness and of space itself.

13. See Steiner, R., *Anthroposophy and the Inner Life* (GA 234), tr. V. Compton-Burnett, London: Rudolf Steiner Press 1992, lecture of 20 January 1924. Also lecture course *Man, Hieroglyph of the Universe* (GA 201), tr. G. & M. Adams, London: Rudolf Steiner Press 1972, lectures of 16 and 17 April 1920.

14. See Polzer-Hoditz, L., *Erinnerungen an Rudolf Steiner* (Memories of Rudolf Steiner), Dornach 1985.

15. Dr Georg Unger is a physicist who led the Mathematical-Astronomical Section of the School of Spiritual Science in Dornach for many years.

16. See Steiner, R., *Polarities in the Evolution of Mankind* (GA 197), London: Rudolf Steiner Press/New York: Anthroposophic Press, 1987, lecture of 30 July 1920.

17. Concerning the time of Atlantis, see Steiner, R., *Occult Science: an Outline* (GA 13), tr. G. & M. Adams, London: Rudolf Steiner Press 1984, and Steiner, R., *Cosmic Memory* (GA 11), tr. K. E. Zimmer, New Jersey: Rudolf Steiner Publications 1971.

18. Steiner, R., *The Philosophy of Spiritual Activity: A Philosophy of Freedom* (GA 4), tr. rev. R. Stebbing, Forest Row, Sussex: Rudolf Steiner Press 1992, Chapter XII.

19. This question arose from a lecture given by the author in Hamburg on 11 November 1992 on the theme 'Zeitgeschehen im Lichte der Apokalypse' (Signs of the Times in the Light of the Apocalypse). In regard to this whole theme, see the Revelation of St John, and Steiner, R., *The Apocalypse of St John. Lectures on the Book of Revelation* (GA 104), tr. rev. J. Collis, London: Rudolf Steiner Press 1977.

20. Steiner, R., *Cosmosophy* (GA 207), tr. A. Wulsin, New York: Anthroposophic Press 1985, lecture of 23 September 1921.

21. See Revelation, Chapters 2 and 3 (Christ's messages to the seven churches as a depiction of the seven post-Atlantean cultural eras), and Steiner, R., *The Apocalypse of St John*, op. cit., lecture of 20 June 1908.

22. See Steiner, R., *The World of the Senses and the World of the Spirit* (GA 134), tr. R. Mansell, Long Beach, California: Rudolf Steiner Research Foundation 1990, lecture of 27 December 1911.

23. For more about the path of knowledge, see Steiner, R., *Knowledge of the Higher Worlds. How is it Achieved?* (GA 10), tr. rev. D. S. Osmond, C. Davy, London: Rudolf Steiner Press 1976, and Steiner, R., *Occult Science, an Outline*, op. cit.

24. See Steiner, R., *A Road to Self-knowledge. The Threshold of the Spiritual World* (GA 16 and 17), tr. H. Collison, M. Cotterell, London: Rudolf Steiner Press 1975, the chapter headed 'Concerning the Boundary between the Physical World and Supersensible Worlds'.

25. Steiner, R., *Boundaries of Natural Science* (GA 322), tr. F. Amrine, K. Oberhuber, New York: Anthroposophic Press 1987, lecture of 29 September 1920.

26. Steiner, R., *From Symptom to Reality in Modern History* (GA 185), tr. A. H. Parker, London: Rudolf Steiner Press 1976, lecture of 20 October 1918.

27. Steiner, R., *The Occult Movement in the 19th Century* (GA 254), tr. D. Osmond, London: Rudolf Steiner Press 1973, e.g. lecture of 19 October 1915.

28. See Steiner, R., *Boundaries of Natural Science*, op. cit., lecture of 27 September 1920.